PATHWAY TO CHANGE

A GUIDE TO PERSONAL TRANSFORMATION

Second Edition

Martha R. Bireda, Ph.D.

blue ocean press
tokyo

Most blue ocean press are available at special quantity discounts for bulk purchases for sales promotions, premiums, and educational needs. Please contact us for details.

Copyright © 1995, 2007 Martha R. Bireda

All rights reserved.
This publication may not be reproduced, stored in a retrieval system, or transmitted in any form or by any means, electronic, mechanical, photocopying, recording, or otherwise, without prior written permission of the publisher.

Published by:

blue ocean press, an Imprint of Aoishima Research Institute (ARI)
#807-36 Lions Plaza Ebisu
3-25-3 Higashi, Shibuya-ku
Tokyo, Japan 150-0011

mail@aoishima-research.com
URL: http://www.aoishima-research.com

ISBN: 978-4-902837-47-1

Printed in the United States of America

Comments from Past Participants of the Pathway to Change Program

"I liked it mostly because of how it separates truths from myths, and allows us to recognize who we are, our abilities, and how we deserve better in life than what we have been given. As for me, I am only giving my attention to messages that empower me."

M.J.

"I liked all of the modules because they helped me to use my voice and speak up as for as my life is concerned."

J.T.

"How to create a life I desire for myself, that's something I have never done. I never made plans for my life, I just took each day as it came. Not even thinking about where I am headed to or what I want."

B.C.

"I liked the module that deals with life choices; the positive and negative choices, because everything in my life has always been negative. I never held my head up long enough from drinking to be positive, when I did hold my head up from drinking, I never thought about anything. Just to go to work again and wait till the day I am off to start back drinking again."

H.J.

"I was very materialistic, but I found out that's not the way. My spirituality needs feeding too, and without that part, I will never be really whole."

M.J.

"It helped me to realize and understand where a lot of my anger and resentment, and negative actions came from. I finally came to realize that I've been harboring my anger for years and years ever since I was a small child). And, now that I know where my problems originated, I can take the necessary steps that I need to change my life, and utilize my knowledge to change the negative aspects of my life to positive."

D.C.

"I can live a sober life and fulfill my dreams."
"I can live a sober life and fulfill my dreams."

J.D.P.

"Core disempowering and empowering beliefs; this was the one to help me dig down in the core of my heart and bring my hurt to surface. I am dealing with my hurt and pain now. I no longer keep it hidden."

B.T.

"It has helped me to finally see that I do have a purpose in life. I have finally realized that my purpose is about me, and myself. And I must say and can say that I have come a long way, because I am no longer in the dark."

H.J.

"I wish to thank this class for everything it has given me. It has given me my desire to want to live, when as before, I could care less. And if it will work for me, then I know this class can and will touch others, thanks so much for everything."

S.R.

PATHWAY TO CHANGE
GRATITUDE LIST

I owe a debt of gratitude to many people for the success of the *Pathway To Change Program*. First, I must thank Dr. Linda Smith, for having the confidence in me to ask that I develop a curriculum for the Life Skills Grant that the Hillsborough County Sheriff's Office was submitting to the United States Department of Education. Secondly, thank you Jan Bates, Manager of Inmate Programs for the Hillsborough County Sheriff's Office, who has faithfully guided the implementation of the program. Thank you to Anne-Marie Perotti-Marsicano of Inmate Training and Resources, and Joel Pietsch, of Inmate Treatment and Intervention for so effectively supervising the implementation of Pathway To Change. A tremendous amount of gratitude is owed the staff who with much dedication facilitated the program: Linda Beavers, Faye Brown, Rene Davelt, Gerald Dilbeck, Mark Diggs, Joyce Hendricks, Chris Howell, Kenneth Kim, Linda Lafaye, Frank Pressey, Judy Newsome, and Toby Smith.

Finally, thank you to the inmates who participated in the program. and for the encouragement to introduce the program to a wider audience.

Pathway To Change was originally known as *Pathway To Personal Empowerment*.

CONTENTS

Introduction to the Second Edition		11
Pathway To Change: Basic Principles		13
The Path		14
How To Use This Book		15
The Contract		17
Pre-Test		19
Module I:	Who Am I?	21
Module II:	How Did I Get Here?	31
Module III:	Where Am I Going? How Do I Change Course?	43
Module IV:	Understanding Power	59
Module V:	The Empowerment Process	69
Module VI:	Beliefs and Power	81
Module VII:	Messages About Power	91
Module VIII:	Understanding Powerlessness	111
Module IX:	Breaking The Cycle of Powerlessness	119
Module X:	Overcoming The Crisis In Values	137
Module XI:	Being Power	167
Module XII:	Doing Power	181

Module XIII:	Connecting Power	199
Module XIV:	Application of Empowerment Principles	209
Module XV:	Staying On The Path	223
Closure		233
Post-Test		235

INTRODUCTION TO THE SECOND EDITION OF *PATHWAY TO CHANGE*

Pathway To Change came into being in 1995, when Dr. Linda Smith, a professor at the University of South Florida, asked me to Develop an empowerment curriculum as part of a Life Skills Program Grant she was submitting to the United States Department of Education. The Hillsborough County Sheriff's Office was awarded the grant and *Pathway To Change* began as a cognitive behavioral program designed to help offenders learn to think in ways that induce behavioral change, leading to an increased sense of personal responsibility and accountability necessary to begin taking action to change their lives.

The first edition of *Pathway To Change* consisted of 10 modules focusing on how to help offenders understand powerlessness, how to break the cycle of powerlessness, and the process of becoming empowered. The program was expanded to address the sense of victimization that most offenders feel and which often serves as a catalyst for offending.

Since the initial development of the program, we saw a trend in offenders who were suffering from a "crisis in values". These individuals, often incarcerated for drug offenses are alienated from their traditional and cultural values and are making choices based upon a value system motivated by materialism and consumerism. A module was included which addresses values and character development.

The 2007 edition of *Pathway To Change* has been expanded to 15 modules and now includes a module which addresses the issue of spirituality. Research has shown that a recidivism reduction program (which *Pathway To Change* was designed to be) cannot be effective unless it addresses the "spiritual emptiness" experienced by many offenders. Finally, I have introduced the "Empowerment Circle", based on the Mastermind principle as an approach to collective support, encouragement, growth and change.

The core message of this book is that individuals possess the personal power to transform their lives. We are all endowed with gifts and talents, and all have a specific purpose for which these gifts and talents are to be employed. I wrote this book after visting a state prison and being overcome by the absolute waste of human potential. I want the reader to understand that he or she posesses the capacity to reach within and to connect to the tremendous power that we all have to free us of limitations and to make us self-determining. My belief is that if the content of this book has been used successfully with inmates then the principles can be effectively used by any individual who is trapped by personal myths and erroneous beliefs that keep them disempowered.

PATHWAY TO CHANGE
BASIC PRINCIPLES

The basic principles upon which *Pathway To Change* **is founded.**

We have forgotten who we are; our true selves and as such:

We hold erroneous beliefs about ourselves and our capacity to operate in the world.

We make poor choices (self-destructive and often hurtful to others) based on these erroneous beliefs.

When we become *self-realized* **(aware of our true selves), we challenge and change our beliefs, we make choices and behave in ways that empower our lives.**

All human beings with insight, encouragement, and guidance can change.

THE PATH

Self-realization

Knowledge of power dynamics

Belief system change

Character development

Spiritual connection

Tapping inner resources/personal assets

Application of empowerment principles to life arenas

HOW TO USE THIS BOOK

The *Pathway To Change Program* is most effective when utilized in a small group setting facilitated by a certified *Pathway To Change* facilitator. Through the guidance of the facilitator and the group process, participants are brought to great levels of dynamic understanding. The workbook may however, be used independently by one highly motivated to bring about change in his/her life.

The workbook contains 15 modules set up in the following format:

EXPRESSION: Initial feelings about the topic are expressed.

DISCUSSION: Key concepts are presented about the topic.

REFLECTION: The reader/participant examines the topic and her/his life.

AFFIRMATION: Positive beliefs or statements of truth are written and verbalized.

When you have completed this workbook, you will have acquired:

An understanding of the root causes of your beliefs, feelings, choices and behaviors;

A system for modifying or changing negative and self-destructive beliefs;

Strategies for connecting with the Source, tapping your inner resources, and personal assets;

Skills in decision-making, goal-setting, problem-solving, and managing emotions; and

Strategies for applying empowerment concepts to your major life arenas.

It is highly recommended that you keep a journal as part of the *Pathway To Change* process. The journal is a means of expressing your thoughts and feelings, but also can serve as a guide to areas in which you want to grow. Your journal reflects your experience on the "path". It is your "personal" statement about the process; as such you may use narrative, poems, stories, songs, rap, or drawings to express yourself in whatever way you are feeling as you make an entry. The most important thing is that you consistently make "reflective" entries.

THE CONTRACT

I,………………………**understand that I am** undertaking an intensive, guided encounter to further my personal transformation and empowerment.

I,………………………**commit myself to** complete the 15 modules with dedication and diligence.

I,………………………**commit myself to** complete all of the exercises honestly and to write my feelings, thoughts, and experiences consistently in my journal.

I,………………………**am open and receptive** to the path that I am taking.

PRE-TEST

READ EACH ITEM CAREFULLY. Indicate how much you agree or disagree with each statement using the following scale:

1 = Strongly Agree
2 = Agree
3 = Disagree
4 = Strongly Disagree

Do not spend too much time on any item. Be sure to answer every item. Choose the number (1,2,3, or 4) which seems to most nearly express your present feeling about the statement.

_____ 1. I have control over the direction my life takes.

_____ 2. I have options in life.

_____ 3. I dream about a better life for myself.

_____ 4. I have goals for my life.

_____ 5. I can create the life I desire for myself.

_____ 6. I have the personality traits necessary to achieve the goals I set.

_____ 7. I have unique talents and skills.

_____ 8. I have a support system I can depend on when I need help.

_____ 9. I have the ability to make changes in my life.

_____ 10. I am in control of my life.

_____ 11. I feel good when I have control over others.

_____ 12. I expect to be successful in life.

_____ 13. I am limited in what I can achieve in life because of my race.

_____ 14. I am limited in what I can achieve in life because of my sex (gender).

_____ 15. I can break old habits.

_____ 16. I understand why I take certain actions in life.

_____ 17. I am angry most of the time.

_____ 18. I am taking the actions necessary to improve my life circumstances.

_____ 19. I can handle whatever comes in life.

_____ 20. I can imagine a better life for myself.

MODULE I
WHO AM I?

1.1   Expression: Thoughts About Personal Transformation

1.2   Discussion: Self-Realization

1.2(a) Exercise: Naming Me

1.2(b) Exercise: Boundary Breaking

1.2(c) Exercise: About Me

1.3   Reflection

1.4   Affirmation

WHO AM I?

It is often said that if you don't know where you are going, it is no telling where you will end up. Just as important, if you don't know who you are, you can't even begin to know what direction to take.

"Self-realization" or the awareness of self is essential for our personal growth and change.

Who am I?

This is the most important question that you can ask yourself. It's okay not to know the answer or to even struggle to find out who you are. What is essential is that we ask and are willing to do the work necessary to discover who we are.

1.1 Thoughts About Personal Transformation

1. What does "transformation" mean?
___
___
___
___
___

2. What does "personal transformation" mean?
___
___
___
___
___

3. Why did I choose to participate in this program?
___
___
___
___
___

4. At the end of the program, how do I believe I will be different than I am now?

_____
_____
_____
_____
_____

5. What is the issue of greatest concern to you that you would like to have addressed as you go through this program?

_____
_____
_____
_____
_____

PAIR/SHARE: Working with a neighbor, share your thoughts about items #1-5.

WRITE AN I FEEL STATEMENT:
I feel: _____

_____
_____
_____.

1.2 Self-Realization

Self-realization is "self-knowledge from a higher level with clarity of perception". Self- realization is seeing clearly who are; seeing our "true selves". Self-realization is knowing the truth about ourselves. That truth is:

- We are all born "tabula rasa" or clean slate.
- We are each filled with "ultimate potential".
- We are all born with unique gifts and talents that are to be used to fulfill our life purpose.
- We all have the potential to create.
- We can direct our human energy to heal to rejuvenate, renew, transform ourselves.
- We all have the potential to actualize our true selves.
- We are each unique and special human beings.

When we are self-realized, we are aware of:

- Our power to choose how to believe, think, feel, and act.
- Our power to transcend myths, stereotypes, erroneous beliefs, and old ways of being.
- Our motivations; what influences our choices and actions.
- Our life's calling, purpose, mission, and destiny.
- Our access to the great Source.

Our problems arise because we have forgotten who we really are, our true selves. Over the years, we receive messages from our family and society that give us a false view of who we really are. The goal of the *Pathway to Change* program is to clear up this confusion. *Pathway to Change* is an instrument for erasing confusion in your mind about your true self.

1.2(a) Naming Me

1. What is my full name?
   _____.

2. Who named me?
   _____.

3. What does my particular name mean?
   _____.

4. Why was I given this name?
   _____.

5. Think of a particular quality, attribute or personality trait you would like to develop during this program. Now give yourself a name that expresses that quality.
That name would be:

_____.

1.2(b) Boundary Breaking

1. I am..

2. I can...

3. I enjoy..

4. I dislike..

5. I wish...

1.2(c) About Me

1. My greatest joy...

2. My greatest disappointment..

3. My greatest accomplishment......................................

4. My greatest fear...

5. My greatest need...

6. My greatest desire...

7. My best personality trait..

8. My worst personality trait..

9. My best skill or talent..

10. My worst skill or talent..

1.3 Reflection:

Think about and write your reactions to the following statement:

"What is necessary to change a person, is to change his awareness of himself".

To me this means: _____

_____
_____
_____
_____
_____
_____
_____
_____
_____
_____
_____
_____.

1.4 Affirmation

Say and write the following statement three times a day until you believe it to be true for you.

" I am discovering more of my true self everyday."

● MODULE II ●
HOW DID I GET HERE?

2.1 Expression: Thoughts About My "Now"

2.2 Discussion: Factors Influencing My "Now"

2.2(a) Maslow's Hierarchy of Needs

2.2(b) Reactions To Hierarchy of Needs

2.3 Reflection

2.4 Affirmation

MODULE II

In this module, we will look at our "now", or the life situation in which we find ourselves at the moment. The readings, discussion, and exercises will help you to better understand how you came to be at this particular point in your life.

HOW DID I GET HERE?

Each of us creates our own "now". In other words, we each have chosen through our actions, our current life situation. If we are where we want to be at this point in our lives, we are probably agreeing with the statement. If we are not where we want to be, we are probably saying "no way". But if we are honest with ourselves, we will see that each of us made a choice or series of choices that brought us to this point in our lives.

Actually it all started very early. Each of us has experienced a certain set of life circumstances from birth to now. As we grew and reacted to our particular life situations, we developed a set of beliefs.

These beliefs about ourselves and our place in the world over the years have influenced the choices we have made. Our choices of course, determined our actions, and our actions led us to our current life situation or our "now".

2.1 Thoughts About My Now

1. What is your age now? _____.

What vision or dream did you have for your life when you were:
        6 years old?   12 years old? 18 years old?
(What did you think your life would be like now?)

2. When I was 6 years old I _____

_____

_____

_____

_____

_____.

3. When I was 12 years old I _____

_____

_____

_____

_____

_____.

4. When I was 18 years old I _____

_____

_____

_____

_____

_____.

5. As you look at your life now, how did your vision or dream change? _____

_____

_____

_____

_____

_____.

6. What beliefs influence your life now? _____

_____

_____

_____

_____

_____.

7. What choices have you made that have determined your current life situation or your "now"? _____

_____

_____

_____

_____

_____

PAIR/SHARE: Working with a neighbor, share your thoughts about items #1-5?

WRITE AN " I BELIEVE" STATEMENT:

I believe: _____

_____

_____

_____

_____

_____

_____

2.2 Factors Influencing My "Now"

Our beliefs influence our choices; our choices influence our actions; and our actions determine our current life situations.

In our twelve (12) years of work with the *Pathway To Change* program, we have identified four factors that can influence one to make poor or self-destructive choices. All four factors are related to erroneous beliefs about ourselves and our personal power. The four (4) factors are:

A sense of victimization: Feelings of vulnerability, neediness, and being "ungrounded". One regards every disappointment, separation, and loss as something that cannot be controlled or changed.

Sense of powerlessness: Feeling victimized leads to a sense of powerlessness; the belief that one cannot exert influence, effect change, or take control of one's life situation.

Crisis in Values: Occurs when one is disconnected or alienated from one's own cultural or traditional value system; accepts and attaches to materialistic and consumeristic values.

Spiritual emptiness: The belief that material "things" can erase the sense of deep emptiness; lack of knowledge or conscious connection to the Supreme Source; ego or fear dominated.

2.3(a) Maslow's Hierarchy of Needs

1. Human beings have a set of innate needs.

2. These needs are arranged in a hierarchy (pyramid) according to potency or strength.

3. The lower the need on the pyramid the more powerful it is; lower level needs are similar to those possessed by non-human animals.

4. The higher the need, the weaker and more distinctly human it is; only humans possess higher level needs.

5. We feel anxious when the first four needs are not met.

6. When the higher level needs are fulfilled, they do not go away; they motivate us further.

7. To self-actualize or reach our potential is the most "human" thing we can do.

MASLOW'S HIERARCHY OF NEEDS

Self- Actualization
Esteem Needs
Love/Belonging Needs
Safety Needs
Basic/ Physiological Needs

1. **Basic/Physiological Needs:** Biological needs for food, water, air, sleep; once these needs are met, you can concentrate on the second level needs.

2. **Safety Needs:** Need for structure, order, security, stability, protection, and predictability.

3. **Love/Belonging Needs:** Need for a supportive family, friends, companions, intimate relationship, identification with a group, and a sense of community.

4. **Esteem Needs:** Lower level esteem needs are respect of others, need for status, fame, glory, recognition, attention, reputation, appreciation, and dignity; Higher level esteem needs are *self-respect, confidence, competence, achievement, mastery, independence, and freedom.*

5. *Self-Actualization: Awareness of our fullest potential; "to be all we can be", being the most complete, "fullest" you.*

We each have needs basic and being (higher level) that must be met. If our needs remain unmet, than we will be unable to fully actualize or reach our potential. When our needs remain unmet we can develop a sense of victimhood. Because a sense of victimhood can lead to a sense of powerlessness, we may develop a faulty or erroneous set of beliefs about ourselves and our capacity to meet our needs. This belief system may then lead us to make choices based upon a faulty value system. Ultimately, self-actualization is about our connection to the Source. The more disconnected we are from the Source, the more likely we are to make choices based upon erroneous beliefs and faulty values.

2.2(b) Reactions To Hierarchy of Needs

PAIR/SHARE: Working with a neighbor, share your reactions to the following questions:

1. How do people react at each level when their needs are not met? (Consider each level separately)

2. How have you reacted when your needs have not been met? (Consider each level separately)

3. What types of choices do people make when their needs are not met? (Consider each level separately)

4. What positive rather than negative choices can people make when their needs are not met? (Consider each level separately)

WRITE AN "I LEARNED" STATEMENT:
I learned: _____
_____
_____
_____
_____
_____
_____.

2.3 Reflection:

Think about and write your reactions to the four factors that can influence our choices and our "now". How does each apply to you?

1. Sense of victimization: _____
_____
_____
_____.

2. Sense of powerlessness: _____
_____
_____
_____.

3. Crisis in values: _____
_____
_____
_____.

4. Spiritual emptiness: _____
_____
_____
_____.

2.4 Affirmation

Say and write the following statement ten times, three times a day until you believe it to be true for you.

" I am aware of how I create my now."

● MODULE III ●
WHERE AM I GOING? AND HOW DO I CHANGE COURSE?

3.1　Expression: Thoughts About Change

3.2　Discussion: What Change Requires

3.2(a) Exercise: Changing Course

3.2(b) Why People Don't Change (Blocks To Change)

3.2(c) The Change Process

3.3　Reflection

3.4　Affirmation

MODULE III

In this module, we will talk about change, specifically changing our life course. If in Module II, we discovered that we are not where we want to be in life, then it is necessary for us to choose a new path. Choosing a new path will require us to change our beliefs, attitudes, and actions.

WHERE AM I GOING?
HOW DO I CHANGE COURSE?

The Nature of Change

In Buddhism, one of the absolute truths is the truth of *impermanence*. The word impermanence means the state of unceasing change on the path of life. This change can be either positive or negative. According to this thinking, the nature of life, which consists of body, life conditions, actions, mind are all subject to change. These life changes may be large or small, expected or unexpected. Some changes will occur naturally, and other changes will occur because of the choices we make. Happiness, prosperity, success, sorrow, deterioration and failure, etc., are all considered to be the results of changes caused by human actions.

There are two things to remember about change. First, change is certain, and second, we can use the process of change to better our lives.

3.1 Thoughts About Change

Write your thoughts about the following questions:

1. What is change? _____

_____
_____
_____
_____
_____
_____

2. What is the purpose of change in our lives? _____

_____
_____
_____
_____
_____
_____
_____

3. What changes would you like to accomplish as a result of participating in *Pathway To Change*? _____

_____

_____

_____

_____.

PAIR/SHARE: Working with a neighbor, share your thoughts about items #1-3.

WRITE AN "I BELIEVE" STATEMENT:

I believe: _____

_____

_____

_____

_____

_____

_____

_____.

3.2 What Change Requires

Change is a process. This means that change occurs in a set of steps. We start at one point and move through the change process. Change is rarely easy; it takes a lot of hard work. Most of all, our changing takes a commitment to ourselves. It takes our loving and respecting ourselves enough to take a better path. Below is a description of what change requires.

CHANGE IS:

Risky

Fearful

Demanding

Powerful

1. To change, you must take risks.
You will not know the results until you get into the process; you can succeed or fail, but only you can determine the outcome.

2. To change, you have to let go of our fears.
Plain and simple, change is scary. When you choose to change, you are choosing to walk into unfamiliar territory and that can be very frightening. It is the fear of the unknown that makes you fear change.

3. To change, you must exercise self-discipline and work hard.
Change requires self-discipline and hard work. You must "act", you cannot "sit back" and let things happen. Through the process of change, you become an "actor" rather than a "victim".

4. To change, you must tap and use our personal power.
When you change, you create options in your life. You break out of boxes. You are free. As soon as you start to change you know that you are tapping and using your personal power.

3.2(a) Exercise: Changing Course

Respond to the following questions.

1. What "now" has your old path created? _____

_____
_____
_____
_____
_____.

2. Where are you headed if you stay on the old path? _____

_____
_____
_____
_____
_____.

3. If I take a new path, I will _____

_____
_____
_____
_____.

3.2(b) Why People Don't Change

There are many reasons why people do not change but here are five (5) major reasons:

Fear: fear of unknown or the loss of something, friendship, respect, inability to meet needs, etc.

Lack of knowledge: simply not knowing how to change.

Lack of motivation: being stuck in a "rut"; old habits and patterns.

Lack of confidence: no belief in oneself that he/she can do the work of change.

Lack of self-love/self-respect: the belief that one does not deserve any better in life.

PAIR/SHARE: Working with a neighbor, complete the following exercise.

Take a few minutes to consider what you must do in order to make a change in your life.

1. What barriers or blocks to change do I face? _____

_____

_____

_____

_____.

2. What people or things can help me to change? _____

_____

_____

_____

_____

_____

_____.

3.2(c) The Change Process

Three elements are necessary for you to if you are to successfully engage in the process of change. As you work through the Pathway To Change program you will master each of the these three crucial areas.

To change you must have:

> Awareness: of self; your beliefs, values, attitudes, fears, needs, gifts, talents, etc.
>
> Knowledge: of how to change; power dynamics, how to apply empowerment principles, etc.
>
> Skills: needed for empowerment; to design a life plan, etc.

3.3 Reflection

Think about your life in the last 12 months.

1. What changes have occurred in your life? _____

_____
_____
_____
_____
_____
_____.

2. What are naturally-occurring changes (growing older, children starting school or leaving home, etc.) _____

_____
_____
_____
_____
_____
_____.

3. What changes have occurred in your life because of the choices you have made? _____

_____

_____

_____

_____

_____

_____.

4. What changes that have occurred in your life have pleased you?

_____

_____

_____

_____

_____

_____

_____.

5. What changes that have occurred in your life do you regret?

_____

_____

_____

_____

_____

_____

_____

_____

3.4 Affirmations

Say or write either or all of the following statements ten times, three times a day, until you believe them to be true for you.

" I choose to change my life".
"I am ready to change my life."
"I am changing my life."

MODULE IV
UNDERSTANDING POWER

4.1   Expression: Thoughts About Power

4.2(a) Discussion: Key Terms

4.2(b) Discussion: Four Ways of Achieving Power

4.3   Reflection

4.4   Affirmation

MODULE IV

In this module, we will begin our discussion of *power dynamics*. Power dynamics influence every aspect of our lives. Understanding what power is, and how it operates in our lives, allows us to make better choices and to express greater control over our lives.

UNDERSTANDING POWER

According to William Glasser, M.D., people are driven by six basic needs. He believes that all of our choices and behaviors are based upon our need for survival, love, belonging, freedom, fun, and POWER. He also feels that 95% of all discipline problems are the misguided efforts of children to try to achieve some sense of power.

SOME BASIC CONCEPTS ABOUT POWER:

Power is a basic human need.

Many of our actions are directed towards experiencing a sense of personal power.

We attempt to meet our power needs in both healthy constructive ways and unhealthy destructive ways.

4.1 Expression: Thoughts About Power

Take just a few minutes to think about each question, then write your reactions to each question.

1. What is power? _____
_____
_____
_____
_____.

2. Who has power? _____
_____
_____
_____
_____.

3. How does one get power? _____
_____
_____
_____
_____
_____.

4. How can understanding power change my life? _____

_____

_____

_____

_____

_____

_____.

4.2(a) Discussion: Key Terms

POWER: the ability to act, do, or produce; **to determine the conditions of one's life.**

POWERLESSNESS: the belief that one cannot exert influence, effect change, or take control of one's life situation.

EMPOWERMENT: The process through which individuals develop options and gain greater control over their lives.

DISEMPOWERMENT: A process by which individuals lose control of their lives.

4.2(b) Discussion: Four Basic Sources of Power

Power comes from four basic sources:

    Being: our inner resources

    Doing: our capabilities; use of skills and talents

    Connecting: uniting with others for some purpose

    Domination: controlling, oppressing, exploiting others

Being, doing, and connecting with others for positive purposes is the constructive use of power.

Connecting with others for negative purposes and dominating others is the misuse and abuse of power (destructive use of power).

Power in itself is not bad or negative; it is only the misuse of abuse of power that causes problems for ourselves and others. The misuse or abuse of power will always ultimately create conflict and problems.

PAIR/SHARE: Working with a neighbor, share your reactions to the following:

1. Describe a situation when you experienced power by "being".

_____
_____
_____
_____
_____

2. Describe a time when you experienced power as a result of "doing".

_____
_____
_____
_____
_____

3. Describe a situation when you experienced power as a result of connecting with others for a positive purpose.

_____
_____
_____
_____
_____

4. Describe a situation when you experienced power as a result of connecting with others for a negative purpose.

_____

_____

_____

_____

_____

5. Describe a time when you misused or abused power.

_____

_____

_____

_____

_____

WRITE AN "I LEARNED" STATEMENT:

I learned: _____

_____

_____

_____

_____

_____

4.3 Reflection

Keep a Daily Power Journal until the next session. Rate yourself each day on a scale of "0" to "10"; with "0" being feelings of total powerlessness, and "10" being very powerful feelings.

1. What made you feel powerless? _____

_____

_____

_____

_____

_____

_____

_____.

2. What made you feel powerful? _____

_____

_____

_____

_____

_____

_____

_____.

4.4 Affirmation

Say and write the following statement ten times, three times a day until you believe it to be true for you.

" I am meeting my power needs in positive and constructive ways."

● MODULE V ●
THE EMPOWERMENT PROCESS

5.1 Expression: Thoughts About Empowerment

5.2(a) Discussion: The Empowerment Process

5.2(b) Exercise: Preparing For Empowerment

5.3 Reflection

5.4 Affirmation

MODULE V

In this module, we will talk about how to move from a life situation of dis-empowerment to a state of empowerment. The path to empowerment begins with becoming aware of and changing our beliefs where necessary.

THE EMPOWERMENT PROCESS

Empowerment is a process. It occurs over a period of time and involves two aspects: **awareness** and **action.** Empowerment involves our becoming increasingly aware. We become aware of who we truly are (our true selves), and the influences that affect our lives. Empowerment also requires action. Through unlearning, learning, and sometimes relearning, we discover the sources of our personal power and use that power to create the lives that we desire. Empowerment is the process that you will use to change your life.

5.1 Thoughts About Empowerment

Respond to the following statements.

1. I feel that empowerment _____

_____

_____

_____

_____.

2. I believe that I can become empowered if I: _____

_____

_____

_____

_____.

3. The changes I that I will see in my life when I become empowered are: _____

_____

_____

_____

_____.

5.2(a) The Empowerment Process

Becoming empowered requires your awareness of the *erroneous* beliefs that you hold and taking the action necessary to change those beliefs. Our beliefs are what we feel is true. Erroneous beliefs are beliefs based on incorrect information. Below are five steps that are involved in the empowerment process.

Understand the power of your beliefs: Beliefs precede (come before) behavior. We can pay attention to and change our beliefs. If we change our beliefs, we can

Identify disempowering beliefs: We must be able to change our behavior and identify those beliefs that we hold that cause us to lose our personal power.

Challenge disempowering beliefs: We must question the truth of the beliefs; then refute or prove them wrong.
We must always ask: Why does this belief lead me?

Adopt a new belief system: It is essential that we develop new ways of thinking.

Act upon your new empowering beliefs: If we think differently, then we will act differently. If we behave in the same way, then we haven't changed our beliefs.

5.2(b) Preparing For Empowerment

Answer the following questions as you prepare to begin the empowerment process.

1. What do I believe about my ability to change my life? _____

_____
_____
_____
_____
_____
_____
_____.

2. How do I know I am willing to make changes in my beliefs and attitudes?_____

_____
_____
_____
_____
_____
_____
_____.

3. What beliefs do I hold about myself that have brought me to my current life situation? _____

_____

_____

_____

_____

_____.

4. What makes me think that I am willing to experience the discomfort involved in challenging long-held beliefs? _____

_____

_____

_____

_____

_____.

5. What new beliefs and ways of thinking do I feel will lead to to positive changes in my life? _____

_____

_____

_____

_____

_____

_____

_____.

6. Why do I feel that I am willing to experience the fear and discomfort that are a part of trying our new behaviors? What will I fear most? _____

_____

_____

_____

_____

_____

_____.

PAIR/SHARE: Working with a neighbor, share your responses to the six questions asked in the Preparing For Empowerment exercise.

WRITE AN "I FEEL" STATEMENT:
I feel: _____
_____
_____
_____
_____
_____
_____
_____.

5.3 Reflection

Imagine that you have the power to create the life that you desire for yourself. What would your life be like?

Use the eight life arenas as a guide.

        Spiritual

        Career

        Education

        Intimate Relationships

        Family Relationships

        Health

        Leisure

        Community

Use this page to describe the life that you would create.

5.4 Affirmation

Say and write the following statement ten times, three times a day until you believe it to be true for you.

" I am taking the actions necessary to increase my personal power."

MODULE VI
BELIEFS AND POWER

6.1 Expression: Thoughts About Beliefs

6.2(a) Discussion: Core Beliefs
Disempowering Beliefs
Empowering Beliefs

6.2(b) Exercise: Challenging Disempowering Beliefs

6.2(c) Discussion: The Truth About Me

6.3 Reflection

6.4 Affirmation

MODULE VI

The first step involved in the empowerment process is to understand the power of our beliefs. In this module, we will look closely at what we believe about ourselves. We will begin the work of challenging and changing those beliefs that are blocks to our reaching our highest potential.

THE POWER OF BELIEFS

A belief is what we think or feel to be true. Our beliefs are formed early in our lives. We learn them from people we love and respect such as our parents, family members, friends, and peers. Unless the cycle is broken, beliefs are passed from one generation to another. We also learn other beliefs from society and powerful others such as authority figures and the media.

Beliefs are quite powerful; they determine what we do, feel, and experience. Our beliefs influence how we see the world. The determine our actions. Our beliefs can enlarge or limit the options that we have in life.

We will usually achieve in life what we believe we will achieve. In other words, our beliefs will create the life that we will experience.

6.1 Thoughts About Beliefs

Have you ever taken the time to think about what you believe to be true about you. Write your beliefs about you in the spaces provided below. Write as much as you can for each item.

I AM: I AM NOT:

I CAN: I CAN NOT:

I WILL: I WILL NOT:

6.2(a) Discussion: Core Beliefs

There are two types of beliefs that we can hold about ourselves: disempowering beliefs and empowering beliefs.

Disempowering beliefs limit our options in life. They cause us to act in self-defeating ways. Unfortunately, many of us hold disempowering beliefs about ourselves. Empowering beliefs on the other hand, create options and possibilities in our lives. They help us to act in self-enhancing ways.

CORE DISEMPOWERING BELIEFS

If we hold these three beliefs about ourselves and act on them, we will live our lives as victims.

I am inferior/less than/not good enough.
I don't deserve more in life.
I am helpless to change my life.

CORE EMPOWERING BELIEFS

If we hold these three beliefs about ourselves and act on them, we can create the lives that we desire.

I am worthy/good enough.
I deserve the best that life has to offer.
I have the ability to change my life.

6.2(b) Challenging Disempowering Beliefs

Think of a time when you may have held each of the disempowering beliefs (stated above) about yourself. Go back to your childhood.

1. A time when I felt inferior to, less than others or not good enough was when: _____

_____
_____
_____
_____
_____
_____.

2. A time when I felt like I didn't deserve to have something good or better in my life was: _____

_____
_____
_____
_____
_____
_____.

3. A time when I felt hopeless or that I could not change the conditions of my life was: _____

_____

_____

_____

_____

_____

_____

_____

_____

_____

_____.

PAIR/SHARE: Working with a neighbor, complete the exercise that follows:

Disempowering beliefs can also be called "erroneous" beliefs. This means that they are in error; they are false, not true. Challenge each of the disempowering beliefs from the exercise above using the statements below.

> Why did I believe this to be true of me?
> How did I develop this belief?
> Why is this belief untrue for me?
> What is the truth about me?

WRITE AN "I LEARNED" STATEMENT:
I learned: _____

_____
_____
_____
_____
_____
_____
_____
_____
_____.

6.2(c) The Truth About Me

Consider these truths about each of us as a human being:

I am a unique and special person.

I have a special purpose to fulfill in my life.

I possess the inner resources to help me fulfill my life purpose.

I have the power to transform my life.

6.3 Reflection

How have my beliefs influenced the path that my life has taken? Have most of my actions been based upon empowering or disempowering beliefs?

_____
_____
_____
_____
_____
_____.

6.4 Affirmation

Say and write the following statement ten times, three times a day until you believe it to be true for you.

" **I am changing my life by changing my beliefs.**"

● MODULE VII ●
MESSAGES ABOUT POWER

7.1 Expression: Thoughts About Messages

7.2(a) Discussion: Two Kinds of Messages

7.2(b) Discussion: Messages From Family

7.2(c) Discussion: Messages From Peers

7.2(d) Discussion: Messages From Society

7.2(e) Exercise: Stereotyping and Labeling

7.3 Reflection

7.4 Affirmation

MODULE VII

In this module, we will talk about the kinds of messages that influence the beliefs that we form about ourselves. If we can understand how we came to believe as we do, we can undo or unlearn some of the erroneous or mistaken beliefs that we hold about ourselves.

MESSAGES ABOUT POWER

The messages that we receive about power and our relationship to it, come from three major sources: our family, our peers, and the society at-large.

The earliest messages that we receive that tell us about about ourselves and our place in the world come from our family.

As we leave our home base (family) and venture out into the world, we receive messages from our peers in the neighborhood and at school that influence how we view ourselves. Finally, we are constantly receiving messages about our members of our race, ethnic group, and social (class) group from the larger society.

We get messages from the media, politicians and our

public servants, even our teachers. Finally, the condition or situation in which we live sends powerful messages that help determine what beliefs you will form about your potential to experience power in your life.

7.1 Thoughts About Messages

Think about the messages have you learned about your personal power and the power of people like you (your race, ethnic, social group). Remember power is the ability to act, do, or produce; to determine the conditions of one's life. Messages that you received early on about you personally ultimately help to determine what you will believe about your ability to exercise power in your life.

1. What is one message that you received about you personally that determined your beliefs about power? _____

_____

_____

_____

_____

_____

2. What is one message that you received about your group that influenced your beliefs about power? _____

_____

_____

_____

_____

7.2(a) Two Kinds of Messages

We generally receive to kinds of messages that help us to form our beliefs about ourselves and our power to determine the course of our lives. We either receive *empowering* or dis*empowering* messages from our families, peers, and the larger society.

Empowering messages are based on "truths" about our human potential. They help us to develop beliefs that encourage our tapping and using our personal power. These beliefs lead to the discovery of options for our lives.

Disempowering messages are based on myths, stereotypes, and misinterpretations of experiences. The beliefs developed from disempowering messages limit our ability to tap and use our personal power. These beliefs lead to a life pattern with limited options.

7.2(b) Messages From Family

We begin early on to receive messages from our parents and other family members about our worth and our potential. Unfortunately, for too many of us, the first messages that we receive about ourselves are disempowering. Some of the disempowering messages that we hear early in our lives influence what we come to believe about ourselves are stated below:

" You are just like your no good daddy/mama.'
"You are never going to amount to anything".
" You are stupid."

Each of the messages above helps us to form the belief that we are worthless and that we will never have the power to determine what happens in our lives.

Write some other disempowering messages that you have heard:

1. _____

_____

_____

_____

_____.

2._____
_____
_____
_____
_____.

3. _____
_____
_____
_____
_____.

7.2(c) Messages From Peers

Many of the beliefs that we form about ourselves come from our peers. We want to be like and accepted and the messages that we receive from our playmates and schoolmates influence if we will believe that we are likable and approved of by others.

The messages that we receive from our peers in particular will influence not only what we believe about ourselves, but also what actions we believe we must take in order to be accepted. Some of the negative messages that we receive that influence both our beliefs and behaviors are below:

> " You're a chicken."
> "You're a geek/nerd".
> " You are trying to be white/black, etc."

What are some other disempowering messages that you have heard from peers?

1. _____

_____

_____

_____

_____

_____.

2. _____
_____
_____
_____
_____
_____.

3. _____
_____
_____
_____
_____
_____.

7.2(d) Messages From Society

Some of the most powerful messages that we receive, that help us to form our beliefs about ourselves and our personal power comes from the larger society. Based upon our race, ethnic group, or social class, the messages that we receive influence us to form beliefs such as:

"We don't belong".
"We are not valued".
"We are inferior".

The disempowering messages that we get from society are based on beliefs called "ism's".

ISM'S:

are erroneous beliefs;
are based upon myths and stereotypes;
put us in a box;
limit our potential;
limit our power;
prevent us from meeting our needs;
give us a false picture of reality;
negative impact our relationships with others.

FIVE COMMON ISM'S

Racism: the belief that one's race is superior and the other's is inferior.

Sexism: the belief that one's sex or gender is superior and the other's is inferior.

Ethnocentrism: the belief that one's ethnic group is superior and the other's is inferior.

Classism: the belief that one's social class is superior and the other's is inferior.

Colorism: the belief that one's color is superior and the other's is inferior.

What are some messages that you have heard based upon the "ism's" above?

1. _____
_____
_____
_____.

2. _____
_____
_____
_____.

3. _____
_____
_____
_____.

4. _____
_____
_____
_____.

5. _____
_____
_____
_____.

PAIR/SHARE: Working with a neighbor, share your reactions to the messages received from family, peers, and society.

WRITE AN "I FEEL" STATEMENT:

I feel: _____
_____
_____
_____
_____
_____
_____.

7.2(e) Stereotyping and Labeling

Below is a list of adjectives or labels used to describe members of various ethnic or cultural groups. In the space provided, write the group that you have most often heard associated with the label listed.

KEY: AF = African Descent   EU = European Descent
      EA = East Asian Descent   LA = Latino
      IA = Indigenous American   ID = Indian Descent
           (Native American)   (Asian)
      JW = Jewish   MS = Muslim
      PI = Pacific Islander   CH = Christian

Add any other ethnic or cultural group that you desire:

_____   _____   _____

1. Smart _____

2. Pushy _____

3. Lazy _____

4. Sneaky _____

5. Violent _____

6. Polite _____

21. Athlete _____

22. Industrious _____

23. Disciplined _____

24. Culturally Deprived _____

25. Irresponsible _____

26. Intellectual _____

7. Quick-tempered _____

8. Dirty _____

9. Inferior _____

10. Money-Hungry _____

11. Devout _____

12. Sharing _____

13. Forgiving _____

14. Respectful _____

15. Adventurous _____

16. Immoral _____

17. Shrewd _____

18. Exploitative _____

19. Selfish _____

20. Primitive _____

27. Emotional _____

28. Loud _____

29. Musical _____

30. Strong _____

31. Superior _____

32. Intolerant _____

33. Happy-Go-Lucky _____

34. Peaceful _____

35. Carefree _____

36. Unethical _____

37. Weak Constitution _____

38. Child-like _____

39. Promiscuous _____

40. Dominating _____

WRITE AN "I FEEL" STATEMENT:
I feel: _____

_____

_____

_____

_____

_____

_____

PAIR/SHARE: Working with a neighbor, share your reactions to the stereotypes and labels of other ethnic and cultural groups, as well as your own, received from family, peers, and society. Write some of these comments down.

_____

_____

_____

_____

_____

_____

_____

7.3 Reflection

We often internalize or start to believe the disempowering messages and erroneous beliefs about our racial, ethnic, gender, or social group.

When we start to believe what others (especially the larger society) believes about us; we start to conform or act in ways to fit the stereotype.

Think about negative behaviors or actions in which you have engaged.

Which stereotypes of your group do they fit?

Negative Behaviors	Stereotypes
………………………	………………………
………………………	………………………
………………………	………………………
………………………	………………………
………………………	………………………
………………………	………………………
………………………	………………………

How do you feel about reinforcing or making the stereotype of your group a reality for others? How does your behavior perpetuate or make the stereotype last in the minds of others?

_____

_____

_____

_____

_____

_____

_____

_____

7.4 Affirmation

Say and write the following statement ten times three times a day until you believe it to be true for you.

" I am only giving my attention to messages that empower me."

● MODULE VIII ●
UNDERSTANDING POWERLESSNESS

    8.1   Thoughts About Powerlessness

    8.2   Discussion: Reactions to Powerlessness

    8.3   Reflection

    8.4   Affirmation

MODULE VIII

In this module, we will talk about powerlessness; what happens to us when we become disempowered and how we react. Our goal is to be able to overcome the sense of powerlessness that we might feel. In order to do that, we must first understand what powerlessness is.

UNDERSTANDING POWERLESSNESS

Powerlessness is the belief that we cannot exert influence, effect change, or take control of our life situation.

Certain life conditions or situations can lead us to feel powerless. We are unable to meet our needs or provide for those we love, we may feel powerless. When we lack the skills and knowledge that we feel are necessary to improve our lives, we may feel a sense of powerlessness. When we are trapped in a cycle of self-destructive habits and actions, we may feel powerless to turn our lives around. The ultimate sense of powerlessness is felt when we lack the freedom of physical movement; when someone or something else controls our lives.

8.1 Thoughts About Powerlessness

All of us have felt powerless at some time in our lives, it may have been a significant event or something as simple as getting locked out of our car.

Think about a time in your life when you believed that you had no options, when things seemed hopeless. What did you think? How did you feel?What actions did you take? Write you thoughts under the "THOUGHTS" column; your feelings under the "FEELINGS" column, and the actions you took under the "ACTIONS" column.

THOUGHTS	FEELINGS	ACTIONS
……………….	……………….	……………….
……………….	……………….	……………….
……………….	……………….	……………….
……………….	……………….	……………….
……………….	……………….	……………….
……………….	……………….	……………….
……………….	……………….	……………….
……………….	……………….	……………….
……………….	……………….	……………….
……………….	……………….	……………….

8.2 Reactions To Powerlessness

There are predictable feelings and behaviors that result from feelings of powerlessness. Below are listed common feelings and behaviors.

FEELINGS

Discomfort	Guilt	Anger
Insecurity	Hostility	Resentment
Anxiety	Pain	Exhaustion
Frustration	Inferiority	Hopelessness
Helplessness	Depression	Fear
Shame	Incompetence	Self-hatred

BEHAVIORS

Distrust	Withdrawal	Suspicion
Defensiveness	Hypersensitivity	Violence
Paranoia	Opposition	Clannishness
Fighting	Manipulation	
Dominating Others	Passive-Aggressiveness	

MOST COMMON REACTIONS TO POWERLESSNESS

The most common feeling that results from the experience of powerlessness is **anger.** The most common behavior is

TURNED INWARD
(Hurt Self)
Illness (Psychosomatic)
Depression
Low Self-esteem
Substance Abuse
Self-destructive/risky behavior
Suicide

TURNED OUTWARD
(Hurt Others)
Aggression (verbal/physical)
Violence

PAIR/SHARE: Working with a neighbor share your thoughts and feelings about the reactions to powerlessness.

WRITE AN "I FEEL" STATEMENT:
I feel: _____
_____
_____
_____
_____
_____
_____.

8.3 Reflection

Think again about a time when you felt powerless. What did you **believe** about yourself and your situation? Were your actions based upon empowering or disempowering beliefs?

Explain.

_____
_____
_____
_____
_____
_____
_____
_____.

8.4 Affirmation

Say and write the following statement ten times three times a day until you believe it to be true for you.

"I release all the beliefs that make me feel powerless."

● MODULE IX ●
BREAKING THE CYCLE OF POWERLESSNESS

9.1   Expression: Thoughts About Powerlessness

9.2(a) Discussion: The Cycle of Powerlessness

9.2(b) Discussion: Choicepoints

9.2(c) Discussion: Challenging Negative Thoughts

9.2(d) Empowering Actions

9.3   Reflection

9.4   Affirmation

MODULE IX

In order to experience real power in our lives, we must break the cycle of powerlessness.
In this module, we will talk about how to break old thought patterns so that we can change our lives.

BREAKING THE CYCLE OF POWERLESSNESS

Breaking the cycle of powerlessness is not an easy job. We have to overcome years of disempowering messages from our family, peers, and society. The effect of so many years of being told that we were not worthy, less than, and inferior, is that we come to believe that we really are powerless. Unfortunately, some of us start to act in self-destructive ways that only serve to keep us disempowered. We reach a point however, at which we can choose to remain powerless or to change our lives so that we can experience a sense of personal power. **This is that point for you.** If you choose to change, you will break the cycle of powerlessness; if you choose not to change, you will continue the cycle and even pass it on to your children.

9.1 Thoughts About Powerlessness

Take a few minutes to think about the following question, then write your response below. What prevents me from experiencing more power in my life?

_____
_____
_____
_____
_____
_____
_____
_____
_____
_____
_____
_____
_____
_____
_____
_____.

9.2(a) The Cycle of Powerlessness

Birth: We are all born with the potential to have positive experiences of power in our lives. Babies come into the world, "tabula rasa" with a "clean slate". We ultimately become what is written on that slate as we grow.

Socialization or Conditioning: We are taught what to believe about ourselves and our place in the world. We develop beliefs from the messages that we receive from our parents, relatives, peers, etc. These messages start to shape our beliefs.

Reinforcement: These early messages are proven to be true (even if they are in reality untrue) by society at large. The media and other societal institutions (schools, churches, legal system, political system, economic system, etc.) help to create images of what we believe about ourselves.

Experiences: We have experiences usually shaped by the images held of us or messages we received that further convince of us the truth about us (even if untrue). As children, we are unable to filter out the error from the truth. We believe it all!

Emotional Response: Based on our experiences and the messages we receive, we start to feel in certain ways. Since our beliefs about ourselves are often based on untruths and errors, we begin to feel inferior, helpless and hopeless. The worse we feel about ourselves, the more we believe the untruths; the worse we feel.

Actions: The choices that we make and the actions that we take in life result from the beliefs that we hold about ourselves and our ability to determine what happens in our lives. We can either make choices and take actions that empower us or disempower us.

9.2(b) Choicepoints

In order to fully experience our personal power and to reach our highest potential, we must break the cycle of powerlessness. Powerlessness is a vicious cycle that if not broken by us, we will pass on to our children. We will send them the same erroneous messages and teach them the same untruths that we believe.

Fortunately, all of us have **choicepoints** in our lives. These are opportunities for us to break old patterns and to start anew. When we take advantage of a choicepoint in our lives, we develop new beliefs, learn new ways of behaving, and create options in our lives.

When we free ourselves from the cycle of powerlessness, we free our children and future generations as well.

It is important to remember, however, that in order to break the cycle of powerlessness, it is not enough to change our behavior. We must change our belief system and thoughts as well. If we only change our behavior, the results might be temporary, and we can possibly relapse. If we change our beliefs, then we effect a permanent change that not only affects our present behavior but our future lives as well.

PAIR/SHARE: Working with a neighbor, share your reactions to the comments about each of the stages of the cycle of powerlessness:

1. Birth _____
_____
_____
_____
_____
_____
_____
_____.

2. Socialization/Conditioning _____
_____
_____
_____
_____
_____
_____
_____.

3. Reinforcement _____
_____
_____
_____
_____
_____.

4. Experiences _____
_____
_____
_____
_____
_____.

5. Emotional Response _____
_____
_____
_____
_____
_____
_____.

6. Actions _____

_____

_____

_____

_____

_____

_____

_____.

7. Choicepoint _____

_____

_____

_____

_____

_____

_____

_____.

WRITE AN "I FEEL", "I LEARNED" AND "I BELIEVE" STATEMENT:

I feel: _____

_____

_____

_____

_____

_____.

I learned: _____

_____

_____

_____

_____

_____.

I believe: _____

_____

_____

_____

_____

_____.

9.2(c) Changing Negative Thoughts

Becoming empowered is a process that requires hard work and effort. One of our most difficult tasks will be to monitor and challenge negative thoughts that can lead to a return to negative patterns of unhealthy and self-destructive behavior.

Challenging negative thoughts and replacing negative thoughts with positive ones will help you to avoid falling into old patterns of behavior that keep you disempowered. Use the steps below to help you challenge and replace negative thoughts.

Challenge negative thoughts by asking:
From what disempowering belief does this thought come?
What negative feelings will occur if I continue to think this way?
What are the negative or disempowering actions that can occur if I continue to think this way?
What is the potential negative impact on my life if I give in to these thoughts?

Replace the negative thought with a positive thought:
With what positive or empowering thought can I replace the negative thought?
What positive feelings does this thought bring?
What positive or empowering actions can occur from holding or **affirming** this positive thought?
What will be the potential impact on my life if I hold or **affirm** this positive or empowering thought?

9.2(d) Empowering Actions

Being able to identify feelings that lead to unhealthy and self-destructive actions is part of our empowerment process. If we can <u>tap</u> and <u>transfer</u> our energy from the negative to the positive, we can increase our options and ways of behaving. Taking positive action will help change your negative feelings into positive ones.

Directions: Indicate the frequency that each feeling occurs for you, then describe an action you will take that <u>taps</u> and <u>transfers</u> your energy for positive and empowering results.

A = Always   O = Often   S = Sometimes   N = Never

_____   1. I am bored.
Action: When I feel this way I will: _____

_____

_____.

_____   2. I feel like a phony.
Action: When I feel this way I will: _____

_____

_____.

_____ 3. I am bored.
Action: When I feel this way I will: _____
         _____
         _____.

_____ 4. I need some "excitement."
Action: When I feel this way I will: _____
         _____
         _____.

_____ 5. I'm afraid of having to take responsibility.
Action: When I feel this way I will: _____
         _____
         _____.

_____ 6. I'm afraid to change.
Action: When I feel this way I will: _____
         _____
         _____.

_____   7. I'm afraid I can't change.
Action: When I feel this way I will: _____
           _____
           _____.

_____   8. I am uncomfortable around straight people.
Action: When I feel this way I will: _____
           _____
           _____.

_____   9. I feel alone and isolated.
Action: When I feel this way I will: _____
           _____
           _____.

_____   10. I am angry.
Action: When I feel this way I will: _____
           _____
           _____.

_____   *11.
Action: When I feel this way I will: _____
                 _____
                 _____.

_____   *12.
Action: When I feel this way I will: _____
                 _____
                 _____.

*Add feelings that you have experienced to this list.

9.3 Reflection

Think about the choices you have made and the actions you have taken over the last year. What choices and actions have led to negative or less than desired consequences in your life? What beliefs influenced these actions and kept you in the cycle of powerlessness?

ACTIONS	BELIEFS
....	....
....	....
....	....
....	....
....	....
....	....
....	....
....	....
....	....

What choices and actions have led to positive or desirable consequences in your life? What beliefs influenced these empowering actions?

ACTIONS   **BELIEFS**

....

....

....

....

....

....

....

....

9.4 Affirmation

Say and write the following statement ten times three times a day until you believe it to be true for you.

" I am breaking the cycle of powerlessness in my life."

● MODULE X ●
OVERCOMING THE CRISIS IN VALUES

10.1	Expression: Thoughts About Character
10.2(a)	Discussion: Cultural Values
10.2(b)	Exercise: Values Survey (A&B)
10.2(c)	Discussion: Values Research
10.2(d)	Discussion: Crisis In Values
10.2(e)	Discussion: 16 Principles of Character
10.2(f)	Life Choices Activity
10.3	Reflection
10.4	Affirmations

MODULE X

We have talked about our beliefs and how they influence our experiences. Our values are equally important. They influence our choices and behavior, and as a result our life experiences as well. In this module we will discuss those values that build good moral character and help us to experience a positive sense of power.

THE POWER OF VALUES

Values are what we consider to be right or important. Our values are a different set of beliefs; they are our moral beliefs and attitudes. Values are our ideas about what is right or wrong, good or bad. Our values are the ideals or principles by which we live; and the goals or what we strive attain. Our values are very powerful because the type of values that we hold influence the strength of our character. Character is moral or ethical strength; integrity. Our character determines our choices and produces the behavior that is beneficial for ourselves, others, our community and society. Good character is a set of positive values that a person both possesses and practices.

10.1 Thoughts About Character

Take a few minutes to think about the following statement, then write your reaction below.

" A man's character will determine his destiny".
Yoruba proverb

_____
_____
_____
_____
_____
_____
_____
_____
_____
_____
_____
_____
_____
_____.

10.2(a) Cultural Values

Our culture provides a framework for our thoughts and actions. Our culture includes our beliefs, values, symbols, ways of thinking, behaving, and communicating. The beliefs and values of our particular culture are our guide to appropriate behavior. Our culture is like water to a fish; just as the fish must live in water to survive, we too must know and understand our cultural values to live the best possible life.

PAIR/SHARE: Working with a neighbor, talk about your "cultural identity". When you have finished join a small group of about six and share what you have learned about yourself and others.

What is your ethnic/cultural background? _____

_____

_____

_____.

What are the major a) beliefs, b) values, c) customs and d) traditions of your ethnic cultural group? _____

_____

_____

_____

_____

_____

_____

_____

_____

_____

_____.

10.2(b) Values Survey (A)

Place each value in order of importance to you by numbering each item 1-22.

VALUE	IMPORTANCE TO ME
Health	....
Wealth	....
Love/Personal Relationship	....
Family	....
Prestige	....
Accomplishments	....
God/Higher Power	....
Cooperating with others	....
Education	....
Freedom/Independence	....
Acquiring things (materialism)	....
Competing with others	....
Self-respect	....
Wisdom	....
Respect for elders	....
Inner harmony	....
Friendship	....
Pleasure	....

PAIR/SHARE: Working with a neighbor, answer the following questions.

1. What were your five (5) highest rated values? _____

_____

_____

_____

_____

_____.

2. Which of the values that you rated highest do you consider to be traditional values learned from your culture? _____

_____

_____

_____

_____

3. Are there values that you rated high, that you feel are not part of your cultural heritage? Which ones? Why? _____

_____

_____

_____

_____.

10.2(b) Values Survey (B)

Which statement is more like what you believe?

A

1. A good life is having peace of mind, good relationships, and connection to a Higher Source and fellow man.

2. Success is best determined by one's spirit, integrity, and character.

3. A person's worth is worth is best measured by his/her wisdom, and contribution to the community.

4. Looking out for self and materialism are better viewed as moral problems.

B

1. A good life is having wealth and material possessions.

2. Success is best determined by what one has or can buy.

3. A person's worth is best measured by thepossessions that he/she has.

4. Looking out for self and materialism are better viewed as life goals.

or appears between each pair.

PAIR/SHARE: Working with a neighbor, discuss the statements that are more like what you believe; tell the reason for your response.

1. _____

_____

_____

2. _____

_____

_____

3. _____

_____

_____.

TWO VALUE ORIENTATIONS

The values expressed in Side A of the Values Survey are higher order values; their focus is on purpose, good character, and service to others; internal means to obtain happiness.

The values expressed in Side B of the Values Survey are lower order values; they focus on self and the acquiring of things, external means to happiness.

10.2(c) Values Research

1. Once people are above poverty levels of income, gains in wealth have no real pay-off in terms of happiness and well-being.

2. When people obtain more money and material goods, they do not become more satisfied with their lives or more psychologically healthy because of it.

3. Aspiring only to have greater wealth or material possessions is likely to be associated with increased personal unhappiness.

4. People with strong materialistic values and desires report more symptoms of anxiety, and are more depressed than those who are less materialistic.

5. People with strong materialistic values and desires watch more television, use more alcohol and drugs, and have poor relationships.

6. Materialistic values create stress and strain (pace of life, work harder, less time with family, maintaining life style, crime, etc.)

7. Materialistic values occur among people who are uncertain about their relationships, self-esteem, competence, and control.

8. Materialistic values are a negative solution to common insecurities and anxieties.

From *Tim Kasser, 2002*

PAIR/SHARE: Working with a neighbor, react to each of the eight statements in the values research.

1. _____
_____
_____
_____.

2. _____
_____
_____
_____.

3. _____
_____
_____
_____.

4. _____
_____
_____
_____.

5. _____
_____
_____
_____.

6. _____
_____
_____
_____.

7. _____
_____
_____
_____.

8. _____
_____
_____
_____.

WRITE AN "I LEARNED STATEMENT:

I learned: _____

_____

_____

_____

_____

_____

_____.

10.2(d) Crisis In Values

If we do not know or have not been taught our **traditional cultural values,** we can suffer from a **crisis in values.** A crisis in values occurs when we are disconnected from our own traditional or cultural value system. We then more easily accept and attach to values of materialism and consumerism. When we are experiencing a crisis in values we place a high emphasis on things. We use things to make us feel better about ourselves and in many cases to have a sense of power over others.

Developing a strong moral character is one way to help us overcome the crisis in values.

PAIR/SHARE: Working with a neighbor, share your reactions to the questions below.

1. Am I now, or have I experienced a "crisis in values"? _____

_____
_____
_____
_____
_____
_____
_____
_____
_____.

2. How has my life been affected by the "crisis in values"? _____

_____
_____
_____
_____
_____
_____
_____
_____.

10.2(e) 16 Principles of Character

These 16 principles of character or **paths to enlightenment** come from the ancient **Ifa Tradition** of the Yoruba people of Nigeria. It is said that knowledge of and contemplation of the verses can bring about " deepness and change". Use these 16 principles as a way to reflect upon your character and to bring about personal change.

1. Whatever degree of material possessions in life, without good character, it is all meaningless; worthless.

_____

_____

_____.

2. Behave gently and with consideration so that you may live and rest quietly in your home.

_____

_____

_____.

3. Strive continually to attain the absolute truth even while experiencing the tribulations of life.

_____

_____

_____.

4. No matter what, we must be skillful. By being skillful we minimize the obstacles in life and maximize our happiness.

_____

_____

_____.

5. Be alert to your shortcomings and weaknesses. Face the real source of your problems.

_____

_____

_____.

6. One's character is that which determines his or her fortune in the world. For the improvement of Life, one must improve his or her character; one must improve his or her behavior.

_____

_____

_____.

7. Do not practice deception or be in the habit of telling lies; be frank and honest in situations.

_____

_____

_____.

8. Stubbornness is not beneficial; listen to the truth about yourself. Do not disregard well-intended advice.

_____

_____

_____.

9. Anger does not do anything for anyone; patience is the parent of good character.

_____

_____

_____.

10. Strive continually to achieve the impossible; struggle endlessly to improve your destiny.

_____

_____

_____.

11. Guard well against dishonorable acts that may ruin your reputation.

_____

_____

_____

12. Learn to act more and react less; reacting based on the ways of others leads to misfortune.

_____

_____

_____

13. The ancients state that it is time we actually live the truth and not merely believe it.

_____

_____

_____

14. Strive to develop gentle and balanced character in order to win the rope of life.

_____

_____

_____

15. Endeavor earnestly to exercise diplomacy in all matters and at all times.

_____
_____
_____

16. Ifa states that we must not meet force with force nor practice bad medicine. We are to sit quietly and exercise spirit.

_____
_____
_____

PAIR/SHARE: Working with a neighbor, share your reactions to the 16 Principles of Character stated above.

WRITE AN "I WILL" STATEMENT:
I will: _____

_____
_____
_____
_____
_____
_____

10.2(f) Life Choices Activity

Below are ten sets of choices that you will have to make in your life. Each choice will determine if you will life your life as an empowered or disempowered person. Choose wisely!

Directions: For each set of choices, ask yourself the following questions:

1. Which did I choose in the past?

2. How did that choice impact my life? (My current situation or condition)

3. How will making the opposite choice change my life?

Choice #1   Courage vs. Cowardice: To Change vs. To Follow Old Patterns

I choose: _____.

The result of the choice is: _____

_____

_____.

A different choice would mean: _____

_____

_____.

Choice #2   Knowledge vs. Ignorance: Searching for Truth vs. Unquestioning Acceptance

I choose: _____.

The result of that choice is: _____

_____

_____.

A different choice would mean: _____

_____

_____.

Choice #3 True Self vs. False Self: Accurate Identify vs. Accepting Stereotypes

I choose: _____.

The result of that choice is: _____
_____
_____.

A different choice would mean: _____
_____
_____.

Choice #4 Origin vs. Power: Acting vs. Reacting

I chose: _____

The result of that choice is: _____
_____
_____.

A different choice would mean: _____
_____
_____.

Choice #5   Leader vs. Follower: Following the Crowd vs. Becoming One's Own Person

I chose: _____.

The result of that choice is: _____

_____

_____.

A different choice would mean: _____

_____

_____.

Choice #6   Responbility vs. Irresponsible: Making Excuses vs. Making Improvements

I chose: _____.

The result of that choice is: _____

_____

_____.

A different choice would mean: _____

_____

_____.

Choice #7　　Persistence vs. Quitting: Hanging In vs. Giving In When the Going Gets Tough

I chose: _____.

The result of that choice is: _____
_____
_____.

A different choice would mean: _____
_____
_____.

Choice #8　　Direction vs. Confusion: Having a Life Plan and Purpose vs. "Drifting" Through Life

I chose: _____.

The result of that choice is: _____
_____
_____.

A different choice would mean: _____
_____
_____.

Choice #9   Cooperation vs. Competition: Working With Others vs. Working Against Others

I chose: _____.

The result of that choice is: _____

_____

_____.

A different choice would mean: _____

_____

_____.

Choice #10   Spirituality vs. Materialism: The Fulfillment of Commitment to Values vs. The Empitness of Things

I chose: _____.

The result of that choice is: _____

_____

_____.

A different choice would mean: _____

_____

_____.

10.3 Reflection

Affluenza is an infectious disease in which one is addicted to having things. When one suffers this disease, "desires and wants" are turned into "needs". Turning desires and wants into needs often results in our making poor choices which lead to unhealthy and self-destructive behavior.

Think about your life and answer the following questions.
1. Am I afflicted with affluenza? Why yes or no?

_____
_____
_____
_____
_____.

2. Have I turned my "desires and wants" into "needs"? When? How?

_____
_____
_____
_____
_____.

3. What was the result of making my desires/wants needs?

_____

_____

_____

_____

_____.

4. How will I balance my desires/wants and my needs?

_____

_____

_____

_____

_____.

10.4 Affirmation

Say and write the following statement ten times three times a day until you believe it to be true for you.

" I am working each day to develop a strong and balanced character."

● MODULE XI ●
BEING POWER

11.1 Expression: Thoughts About My Spiritual Beliefs

11.2(a) Discussion: Spiritual Emptiness and Spiritual Realization

11.2(b) Discussion: Connecting With The Divine Source

11.2(c) Discussion: "Being" Empowerment Methods

11.2(d) Self-Validation Exercise: My "Dozen"

11.3 Reflection

11.4 Affirmation

MODULE XI

As you recall from Module IV, positive power for constructive purposes comes from three sources: being, doing, and connecting.

Being power comes from our inner resources; it is our personal strengths, personality traits, and our character. The most important source of being power is our spiritual nature. In this module, we will discover the personal assets which are a source of our personal power, and explore our spiritual selves.

BEING POWER

Empowerment is a process of personal transformation. It is a process by which we increasingly become aware of our "true" selves. Recent studies have shown that no program designed to transform the human consciousness is complete unless it includes a spiritual component. We are **mind**, **body**, and **spirit**. We cannot make sustained or lasting change without understanding our spiritual nature and connecting with* God, Allah, Jehovah, Spirit, The Creator, the Source, the Supreme Being, called by whatever name you choose. In order to fully tap our being power we must learn how to connect with our Higher Power or Source.

*These names will be used interchangeably in the text.

11.1 Thoughts About My Spiritual Beliefs

Take a few minutes to think about your beliefs about a Higher Power. Write your thoughts below.

_____
_____
_____
_____
_____
_____
_____
_____
_____
_____
_____
_____
_____
_____
_____
_____
_____
_____
_____.

11.2(a) Spiritual Emptiness and Spiritual Realization

When we are in a state of **spiritual emptiness**, we are unaware of our spiritual nature. We look outside of ourselves for something to bring us a sense of happiness, fulfillment, and completion. Oftimes, we seek God in material things, in alcohol, drugs, sex, and other people.

We worship or make gods out of whatever we are using to make up for the emptiness that we feel inside. We attach to and come to believe that we cannot live with that thing.

According to Buddha, **attachment is the cause of all human suffering"**. We cannot achieve our highest goal as humans, which is to reach our fullest potential unless we overcome spiritual emptiness. To overcome spiritual emptiness, we must reach a state of spiritual realization.

Spiritual Realization: Knowledge of your oneness with God, Allah, Jehovah, Spirit, the Creator, the Supreme Being, etc.

Your purpose here is to realize your spiritual potential.

Search out meaning for your life experiences through spiritual realization.

Realization of the presence of Spirit within you and every other human being.

Spiritual realization comes through prayer, meditation, self-discipline and strong determination.

Seek until you find the path to spiritual realization most suited to the spiritual inclination of your heart and mind.

PAIR/SHARE: Working with a neighbor, share your views about spiritual emptiness and spiritual realization.

Spiritual emptiness: _____
_____
_____
_____
_____
_____
_____.

Spiritual realization: _____
_____
_____
_____
_____
_____
_____.

WRITE AN " I BELIEVE" STATEMENT:

I believe: _____

_____

_____

_____

_____

_____

_____

_____

_____

_____.

11.2(b) Connecting With The Divine Source

To achieve spiritual realization, you must have a spiritual experience. What is necessary to have a spiritual experience or to connect with the Divine Source? To connect with the Divine Source you must:

Quiet the mind.
You cannot connect with the Divine Source or hear Allah's guidance if your mind is in a restless, worried state. Use prayer or meditation to quiet the mind.

Surrender to Spirit.
Have faith and be open to receive guidance. Say: " I don't know what to do. You do. I need your help. I am listening."

Ask for guidance.
"How do I…………………………… …"?
"Tell me what to do in this situation………."
"Show me how to……………………….."

Show gratitude.
Give thanks for answered prayer.

11.2(c) "Being" Empowerment Methods

Empowerment is a process that requires continuous work and effort. There are a number of methods that you can use to help in the process of personal empowerment. If you use these methods on a regular basis, you can more easily tap and use your personal power. Consider using one or more of these methods.

Prayer: By believing and trusting in a Higher Power, you can increase your personal power. Through prayer, you can receive guidance and direction for your life.

Meditation: Is a way of "quieting our mind". When quiet our minds, we gain knowledge from a deeper level within. Meditation is used by many to become calmer and to look within in order to develop wisdom and freedom.

Visualization: We can tap our personal power when we use our imagination. One of the first steps in getting what we want in life is to use our mind to see it. It is true that if we can **see** and **believe** it, we can **achieve** it.

Journaling: When we keep a journal, we are able to express our feelings, thoughts, and beliefs. Through this expression, we give voice to our power. Our journals are a good way to see the empowerment process in action…we can see our transformation over time.

Inspirational Reading: Reading the Bible, Koran, and other Holy Books can provide guidance and direction to our lives. Other spiritual books and even biographies can be an inspiration to us as we travel the path to personal empowerment.

Affirmations: Affirmations are positive statements of truth. Said regularly, affirmations can change our thoughts and ultimately our unconscious beliefs. Affirmations are an essential part of the empowerment process.

11.2(d) Self-Validation Exercise: My "Dozen"

Becoming aware of your unique and special qualities is an essential part of learning to **validate** the self. When we are able to know and appreciate our own **inner resources**, we are experiencing our personal power. When our sense of self-worth comes from within, rather than having to be validated things outside of ourselves such as money, cars, jewelry, and other people, we are empowered.

In the section below, describe twelve (12) traits and qualities that make you "special".

1. ………………………………   7. ………………………………

2. ………………………………   8. ………………………………

3. ………………………………   9. ………………………………

4. ………………………………   10. ……………………………

5. ………………………………   11. ……………………………

6. ………………………………   12. ……………………………

PAIR/SHARE: Working with a neighbor, share your "dozen" traits and qualities that make you a special person.

WRITE AN "I FEEL" STATEMENT:

I feel: _____

_____

_____

_____

_____.

11.3 Reflection

Use one of the empowerment methods from 11.2(c) to help you answer the following questions.

1. What "inner resources" will I use to experience more positive power in my life?

_____

_____

_____

_____

_____

_____.

2. What "inner resources" do I want to develop to gain more positive power in my life?

_____

_____

_____

_____

_____

_____.

11.4 Affirmation

Say and write one or more of the following statements ten times three times a day until you believe it to be true for you.

" I am connecting to my Higher Power each day".
"I am receiving guidance from my Higher Power/God/Allah every day".
" I am becoming more……………………………each day".

● MODULE XII ●
DOING POWER

12.1 Expression: Thoughts About My Personal Assets

12.2(a) Discussion: Tapping and Using My Personal Power The 4 "A"s

12.2(b) Discussion: Learning New Skills

12.2(c) Discussion: Keys To Empowerment

12.3 Reflection

12.4 Affirmation

MODULE XII

In Module XI, we discussed "Being "power. We tap our being power by discovering who we are: " I am…….". We tap our doing power by acting or using our gifts, talents, skills, and abilities. In this module, we will explore the personal assets that are the source of our doing power.

DOING POWER

Our doing power is our "I can … ".

The source of our doing power are our capabilities, the things that we can do to give us power. When we discover and use our gifts, talents, skills, and abilities, we are using our doing power. The most difficult part of using our doing power is acknowledging our gifts and talents and then believing that we can use them to experience more power in our lives.

11.1 Thoughts About My Personal Assets

Take a few minutes to think about and answer the questions below. This page should be filled!!!!!!!!!!!

1. What are my strengths? _____

_____
_____
_____
_____
_____
_____
_____.

2. What gifts, talents, skills, and abilities do I possess? _____

_____
_____
_____
_____
_____
_____
_____.

12.2(a) Tapping And Using My Personal Power

One of the truths about you is that you have power within. No one else can empower you, only you can empower you by tapping your own power source. You can increase your personal power by discovering and using your strengths, gifts, talents, skills, and abilities. Your capacity to "do" can help you to achieve the life that you desire.

There are 4 A's that you can use to increase your power.

Acknowledge your personal assets. We all have them. You just have to do the work of identifying yours. Look within and discover your strengths, gifts, talents, skills, and abilities.

Accept your personal assets. Now that you have found these assets, own them. Believe that your are worthy to possess these assets. It is sometimes difficult for us to accept all of the good things about ourselves. Do it!!!!

Affirm your personal assets. Say them out loud. Remind yourself daily of all the good things that you have going for you.

Act upon your personal assets. Use your strengths, gifts, talents, skills, and abilities to create the life that you desire.

PAIR/SHARE: Working with a neighbor, share your answers to the questions below. Don't be shy.

1. What are your strengths?

_____
_____
_____
_____
_____
_____
_____
_____
_____
_____
_____
_____.

2. Now what gifts, talents, skills, and abilities can you add to the list that you began in 12.1 Thoughts About My Personal Assets?

_____
_____
_____
_____

3. Ask your neighbor what personal assets he/she feels you possess. Write them below.

12.2(b) Learning New Skills

Sometimes we need to learn a new set of skills to increase our personal power. When we know how to make good decisions, how to set goals, how to problem solve, and how to manage our emotions we increase our power.

Four Crucial Empowerment Skills
You will need to develop four key skills to increase your personal power. Decision-making, goal-setting, and problem-solving and managing emotions are skills that empowered persons possess and use.

Learning decision-making skills will provide you with more freedom and control over your life. Because you are a good decision-maker, you will develop more options in your life. Ultimately, you will be more satisfied with the choices you make.

When you set and achieve goals you are using your personal power. In setting goals, you are taking responsibility for what happens in your life...you are taking charge of your life. Goal-setting is taking action. When you set goals, you are using your creative energy to create the life that you desire.

We will always face obstacles in life. Problem-solving skills will provide you with the resources to look clearly at problems and come up with workable solutions. When you have good problem-solving skills you increase your options in life. You are no longer stuck in old, destructive patterns.

Problem-solving skills give you the confidence and the freedom to shape your life.

One of the most difficult tasks for many of us is to learn to manage our emotions. We give our power away when we cannot control our fears or our anger. When we learn how to feel, own, express, and release our emotions, we are experiencing a real sense of power.

THE DECISION-MAKING PROCESS

Step 1: Determine the decision to be made.
Step 2: Determine what is important to you and what you want to accomplish.
Step 3: Determine the information that you need to have.
Step 4: Determine the risks involved in choosing each option.
Step 5: Make a choice.
Step 6: Develop a plan for getting what you want.

EVALUATING YOUR DECISIONS

Step 1: Why did you make this decision?
Step 2: What decision was made?
Step 3: What effect will this decision have on your life?
Step 4: Did you consider all options?
Step 5: Did you make a good decision? Why do you think so?
Step 6: Would you make the same decision in the future? Why?

THE GOAL-SETTING PROCESS

Seven questions to ask:

1. What is my goal?
2. Do I believe I can achieve this goal?
3. What personal assets (gifts, talents, skills, abilities) do I have that will help me to achieve this goal?
4. How will I see the results of achieving this goal in my life?
5. Do I choose to achieve this goal?
6. Am I motivated to achieve this goal? Why?
7. Will achieving this goal increase my personal power? How?

THE PROBLEM-SOLVING PROCESS

Step 1: Identify and define the problem.
Step 2: Think of possible solutions.
Step 3: Consider how well each solution will work.
Step 4: Choose the best solution.
Step 5: Try out your solution.
Step 6: Determine how well the solution worked.

MANAGING YOUR EMOTIONS

Follow the following steps especially when you feel fearful or angry.

Step 1: **Acknowledge** and **own** the feeling.
Step 2: **Observe** your thoughts.
Step 3: **Detach/step back** from your feelings.
Step 4: **Ask:** What does this (situation) mean?
Step 5: **Release/let go of** the emotion.
Step 6: **Wait** for the answer to "what does this mean"?
Step 7: **Respond** in a constructive manner.

USING YOUR SKILLS

1. Describe a decision that you must make in your life. Use the steps in the decision-making process to make and evaluate your decision.

_____

_____

_____

_____

_____

_____

_____

_____

2. Decide upon a goal that you would like to achieve soon. Use the goal-setting process to help you set your goal.

_____

_____

_____

_____

_____

_____

_____

3. Identify a problem that you are now facing or will face. Use the problem-solving process to come to a good solution.

_____

_____

_____

_____

_____

_____

_____.

4. Think of a time when you recently have become very angry or very afraid. Go through the steps of managing your emotions. Describe how you think the outcome of the situation could have been different if you had used this approach.

_____

_____

_____

_____

_____

_____

_____.

PAIR/SHARE: Working with a neighbor, share your responses to the decision-making, goal-setting, problem-solving and managing emotions processes.

WRITE AN "I LEARNED" STATEMENT:

I learned: _____

_____
_____
_____
_____
_____
_____
_____
_____
_____
_____
_____.

12.2(c) Keys To Empowerment

After challenging disempowering beliefs, developing new beliefs about yourself, tapping your inner resources, and discovering your personal assets, you are well on your way to personal empowerment and transformation. You can further increase your sense of personal power by tuning into the three keys to empowerment **PDC: Purpose, Direction, and Commitment.**

> **Purpose:** Our destiny as human beings is to fully actualize or reach our highest potential. Our **purpose** is to manifest the destiny for which we were created by using our unique gifts and talents in service to our community and society.
>
> **Direction:** Your **direction** determines your life course or path. It is the steps that you take to achieve or live your life purpose. We are familiar and comfortable with our old life pattern, so when we choose a new life course or path, we must decide the steps or direction we will take.
>
> **Commitment:** Your **commitment** is your dedication to your new life path and achieving or living your purpose. It determines your ability to "stay the course", and to "hang on" when things get tough. Life is never easy, but if you connect to the Higher Power, tap into your inner resources, and use your personal assets, you will find that you have the personal power necessary to achieve despite the odds.

12.3 Reflection

Use one of the empowerment methods from 11.2(c) to help you begin to answer the questions below.

1. What is my life purpose?

_____
_____
_____
_____
_____
_____
_____
_____.

2. What personal assets (strengths, gifts, talents, skills, and abilities) will help me to achieve/live my life purpose?

_____
_____
_____
_____
_____
_____
_____.

3. How do I see my life and the lives of others changing as a result of my "aligning" (achieving/living) myself with my life purpose?

_____
_____
_____
_____
_____
_____
_____
_____
_____
_____
_____.

12.4 Affirmation

Say and write the following statement ten times three times a day until you believe it to be true for you.

" I am using my gifts and talents to achieve my life purpose".

● MODULE XIII ●
CONNECTING POWER

13.1　Thoughts About Connecting

13.2(a) Discussion: Choosing Friends

13.2(b) Discussion: The Empowerment Circle

13.3　Reflection

13.4　Affirmation

MODULE XIII

We have discussed two sources of personal power; being and doing. In this module we will learn about connecting with positive others (we can...) as a means of increasing our personal power. Specifically, we will talk about the value of establishing and being a member of an Empowerment Circle as a way to help you "stay on the path".

CONNECTING POWER

Connecting with others for a common purpose can be a very important source of power. It is through our interactions that we come to know ourselves better, express who were are, and be a support to others. It is important however, to be aware of our own energy and the energy of those we attract into our lives. If we are on the path to empowerment, then we only want to attract people with positive energy. To attract positive people into our lives, we must ourselves, be connected to our Source, believe in our own worth, be of good character, and make choices and behave in ways that enhance our lives and those we encounter.

13.1 Thoughts About Connecting With Others

Take a few minutes to consider the following. Write your reaction below.

" We are like mirrors. We are who we attract into our lives."

_____
_____
_____
_____
_____
_____
_____
_____
_____
_____

13.2(a) Choosing Friends

Our friends and acquaintances, especially significant others can be crucial in either encouraging or discouraging our personal transformation and empowerment. Choosing the right people with who we will spend our time and share our lives is critical if we are to stay on the path. Below are some questions to ask when choosing those that will be close to you.

ASK:
Does he/she seek the guidance of a Higher Power?
Are you uplifted when you are with him/her?
Is he/she on their own path of growth and change?
Is he/she supportive of your new path?
Is he/she achieving/living their life purpose?
Does he/she believe in their own worth?
Does he/she seek fulfillment from their inner resources or from things outside of themselves?
Is she/he free of addictions (alcohol, drugs, gambling, sex)?
Is she/he of good character?
Will your life be better, enhanced because she/he is in it?

PAIR/SHARE: Working with a neighbor, choose a friend, and evaluate your friendship according to the questions above. By the way, you should have answered each question yes, if the person is a positive influence in your life.

WRITE AN "I FEEL" STATEMENT:

I feel: _____

_____
_____
_____
_____
_____
_____
_____
_____
_____
_____
_____
_____
_____
_____
_____
_____
_____
_____
_____.

13.2(b) The Empowerment Circle

The **Empowerment Circle** is based upon the principle that **the combined energies of two or more like-minded people is a source of great power**, and the belief in a **Higher Power/ Intelligence/Consciousness of which we are all part and which guides us if we are open to** receive.

The Empowerment Circle is:
- a collective source of power that will help you to "stay on the path and reach your highest potential

- a small group of like-minded people with a common goal

- united effort to seek Divine Guidance

- a safe environment to express your hopes, dreams, desires, fears

- on-going mutual support and encouragement

- provides an opportunity for self-observation and self-correction

- a circle of people who will believe in you until you are able to believe in yourself

How The Empowerment Circle Operates:
- Two or more persons meet regularly (weekly) for 1-2 hours.
- A "community of equals"; no leader, all facilitate.
- Confidentiality is strictly enforced.
- Not a social group; for purpose of collective guidance and encouragement.
- Start with a prayer or meditation to invite the guidance of the Higher Power.
- Each member shares successes from the week before, goals achieved, or prayers answered.
- All attention is given to the member speaking.
- Each member in turn makes known their request for the week.
- As the request is stated, all others in turn say: "I support you in your request and I know the Creator hears you and your answer is on the way.
- Thank the Creator for the time together, for protection, and blessings.
- Some things members ask for are: release from past hurts/ pain; freedom from addiction; freedom from old self-destructive habits and patterns; health; prosperity; peace of mind; success with employment or career goals; healing/ harmony in relationships with children, parents, family members, or significant others; success with educational goals; improvement of character; understanding a particular situation; knowing or being aligned with one's life purpose.

13.3 Reflection

What does the following verse mean to you?

"For where two or three are gathered in my name, there am I in the midst of them."

Matthew 18:20

_____

_____

_____

_____

_____

_____

_____

13.4 Affirmation

Say and write the following statement ten times three times a day until you believe it to be true for you.

"I am connecting with others of like-mind for a higher purpose".

● MODULE XIV ●
APPLICATION OF EMPOWERMENT PRINCIPLES

14.1　Thoughts About Applying The Principles

14.2(a)　Discussion: Putting The Empowerment Principles Into Practice In My Life

14.2(b)　Discussion: Application of Empowerment Principles To Relationship Issues

14.2(c)　Discussion: Relationship Notes

14.3　Reflection

14.4　Affirmation

MODULE XIV

We have covered a lot of territory as we traveled our new path. Our goal of this path is life transformation and personal empowerment. In this module, we will review the principles we have learned and see how these principles can be applied in our lives. Specifically, we will devote attention to two key areas of our lives: our personal relationships and our careers.

Application of Empowerment Principles

We are now equipped with the *awareness,* knowledge, and *skills* necessary to apply the empowerment principles in all the key areas of our lives. We are *aware* of our beliefs and values; we *know* why we have made some of the choices we have made in the past and how power operates in our lives.

We have learned *skills* related to making decisions, setting goals, and resolving our problems. Most importantly, we have learned out to connect with the Source of our power and to tap our inner resources.

14.1 Thoughts About Applying The Principles

Take a few minutes to think about the following questions and write your responses below.

1. Am I ready to put the empowerment principles into practice in my life? Why do I think so?

_____
_____
_____
_____
_____
_____
_____

2. In which area of my life do I feel most in need of empowerment? Why do I feel this way?

_____
_____
_____
_____
_____
_____
_____

14.2(a) Discussion: Putting The Empowerment Principles Into Practice In My Life

If you remember, there are five steps involved in the empowerment process; these are:

    Understanding the power of your beliefs.

    Identifying disempowering beliefs.

    Challenging disempowering beliefs.

    Adopting a new belief system.

    Acting upon your new belief system.

We assume that you are knowledgeable of and understand the power of your beliefs, therefore we will only address steps 2-5 in the application of the principles of empowerment below. In the application below, we will show how our **awareness, knowledge, and skills** are incorporated into the application. The application below addresses relationships; our goal is to develop emotional independence.

14.2(b) Application Of Empowerment Principles To Relationship Issues

GOAL: To develop a healthy relationship.

AWARENESS: Common disempowering beliefs:
　　　　I am not worthy of love.
　　　　I don't deserve love.
　　　　I am nothing without a mate.
　　　　I need a mate to be happy.
　　　　I need a mate to take care of me.

KNOWLEDGE: I know the **truth** about me.
　　　　I know what to look for in a healthy relationship.

SKILL: Challenge disempowering beliefs.
　　　　That is not true; I am worthy of love; no one can make me believe that I am not; I know and believe in my own worth.

　　　　I do deserve love; all human beings deserve love; I am no different; I deserve love because I am a very lovable person.

　　　　Who says I am nothing without a mate; you must be crazy; I don't need another person to validate me; I validate myself. I am capable of creating a full and satisfying life.
　　　　Come on, who made that rule; I have all the

inner resources to make me a joyful person. I would like to have a mate but I can be happy with or without a mate. I can especially be happy without the wrong mate.

You must be kidding. I am not a baby. I am perfectly capable of taking care of myself. I have the strength, gifts, and talents to create a good life for myself.

NEW BELIEFS: Based on personal resources and personal assets.

I am a special human being who is worth of love.

I am worthy of the best partner and best relationship possible.

I am made in the image and likeness of God, therefore I am love. As such, I deserve the love that I am.

I love and accept myself exactly the way I am. I approve of myself.

I am creating a happy and fulfilled life for myself with or without a mate.

I am a strong person who has the capability to take care of myself.

ACTING ON NEW BELIEFS: Use empowerment resources and new skills.

    I affirm my new beliefs daily.

    I ask the Creator to help me attract the right mate for me.

    I seek guidance from the Creator on becoming the type of person that I want to attract.

    I seek to learn more about healthy relationships.

    I listen to what my "gut", my "inner voice" says about the person to whom I am attracted or who is attracted to me.

14.2(c) Relationship Notes

CHARACTERISTICS OF A HEALTHY RELATIONSHIP

In a healthy relationship, each partner:

- Feels worthy and deserving of being loved.

- Respects and appreciates the individuality of the other.

- Maintains a sense of individuality while sharing with the other.

- Feels free to express needs, desires, and opinions.

- Is supportive of the other without being controlling.

- Feels secure, complete, and valued in his/her own right.

- Is willing to grow and change.

- Is willing to look at her/his own issues.

- Is willing to do the work necessary to heal his/her own hurts so that the relationship can be improved. Feels loved and fulfilled in the relationship.

UNHEALTHY PARTNERS:

- Do not love themselves.
- Give away their power or attempt to experience power by controlling the other.
- Try to change the other.
- Are emotionally dishonest.
- Do not feel secure, complete, or valued without the other.
- Have unrealistic expectations for the relationship.

HEALTHY PARTNERS:

- Have a loving relationship with themselves.
- Maintain a sense of self.
- Feel secure, complete, and valued in their own right.
- Trust, express and experience power over their feelings.
- Have no need or desire to control the other.
- Desire to grow and change to be a better person and partner.
- Usually don't end up with or try to get away from unhealthy partners.

RELATIONSHIP QUIZ

1. Am I the person that I want to attract or the person I want my mate to be?

2. Do I have a loving relationship with myself?

3. Do I know myself?

4. Do I take responsibility for meeting my own needs or security, completeness, and validation?

5. Do I honestly express my feelings and as for what I need and desire in the relationship?

6. Do I take responsibility for my own feelings?

7. Have I given up the need to control others?

8. Do I deal honestly with my own "baggage"?

By the way, when you are ready for a "healthy" relationship, you can honestly answer all of the questions "yes".

14.3 Reflection

Choose one of the following life arenas and apply the empowerment principles:

    Spiritual
    Career
    Education
    Intimate Relationships
    Family Relationships
    Health
    Leisure
    Community

LIFE ARENA: _____

GOAL: _____
_____
_____
_____

AWARENESS OF DISEMPOWERING BELIEFS: _____
_____
_____
_____

KNOWLEDGE: _____

_____

_____

_____

_____

SKILL(S): _____

_____

_____

_____

NEW BELIEFS: _____

_____

_____

_____

ACTIONS BASED ON NEW BELIEFS: _____

_____

_____

_____

14.4 Affirmation

Say and write the following statement ten times three times a day until you believe it to be true for you.

" I am applying empowerment principles in my life".

● MODULE XV ●
STAYING ON THE PATH

15.1 Expression: Thoughts About Staying On The Path

15.2 Discussion/Exercise: Your Road Map

15.3 Relection

15.4 Affirmation

MODULE XV

We have come to the end of the course and we have learned all of the fundamentals to help us to successfully take the path of personal transformation and empowerment.

In this module, we will "put it all together"; we will design a "road map" for our future.

STAYING ON THE PATH

Pathway To Change has equipped you with the *awareness, knowledge,* and *skills* to live an empowered life. You have acquired an awareness of *self*, the factors that influenced your present life situation, and the impact of your beliefs, values, and thoughts. You have gained knowledge of how to change your life, and how power dynamics influence your life.

You have learned skills in identifying and challenging erroneous beliefs, decision making, problem-solving and managing your emotions. Most importantly, you have learnedhow to connect with your Source, tap your inner resources, and use your personal assets.

Finally, you know how to apply everything you have learned to your life arenas.

15.1 Thoughts About Staying On the Path

Take a few minutes to think about the questions below, then write your reactions.

1. What obstacles will you face in staying on the path? _____

_____
_____
_____
_____
_____
_____
_____.

2. What resources will you use to help remove those obstacles from your path? _____

_____
_____
_____
_____
_____
_____
_____.

15.2 Your Road Map

The road map that you design will help you to stay on the path. If you will use everything that you have learned in this course, you will be able to design an effective plan that will help you be successful in living an empowered life. On the pages that follow, design a "road map" for your life from this point. Include each of the items below as part of your map.

- Life purpose

- Life goals

- Beliefs you hold about yourself and your life

- Ways in which you will tap your being, doing, and connecting power

- Inner resources

- Personal assets

- Skills you will learn and practice

- The outcome you expect

1. Life Purpose: _____

_____
_____
_____
_____
_____
_____
_____

2. Life goals: _____

_____
_____
_____
_____
_____

3. Beliefs I hold about myself and my life: _____

_____
_____
_____
_____
_____

4. Ways in which I will tap my being, doing, and connecting power: _____

_____
_____
_____
_____
_____.

5. My inner resources: _____

_____
_____
_____
_____
_____.

6. My personal assets: _____

_____
_____
_____
_____
_____.

7. Skills I will learn and practice: _____

_____

_____

_____

_____

_____

_____.

8. The outcome you expect: _____

_____

_____

_____

_____

_____

_____

_____

_____

_____

_____

_____.

15.3 Reflection

Imagine your life ten years from now. You arrived at a choice point and you chose to follow the path of transformation and empowerment. In the space below, describe what your life will be life.

_____
_____
_____
_____
_____
_____
_____
_____
_____
_____
_____
_____
_____
_____
_____.

15.4 Affirmation

Say and write the following statement ten times three times a day until you believe it to be true for you.

" I am taking the path of transformation and empowerment."

CONGRATULATIONS!

You have completed the *Pathway To Change* program. You now know how power operates in your life. You know the power of your beliefs and how they influence the choices you make and the actions you take.

You have gone through a process of *self-realization*.

You know who you are... the true you. You understand your inner resources and personal assets can help you experience personal power. You know what methods to use and the skills to practice to increase your power.

Finally, you understand how empowering beliefs thoughts, choices, and actions can make the difference in the quality of your life...whether you are a winner or loser in life.

Believe in yourself and believe in the power within and you have the power to create the life that you desire.

POST-TEST

READ EACH ITEM CAREFULLY. Indicate how much you agree or disagree with each statement using the following scale:

1 = Strongly Agree
2 = Agree
3 = Disagree
4 = Strongly Disagree

Do not spend too much time on any item. Be sure to answer every item. Choose the number (1,2,3, or 4) which seems to most nearly express your present feeling about the statement.

_____ 1. I have control over the direction my life takes.

_____ 2. I have options in life.

_____ 3. I dream about a better life for myself.

_____ 4. I have goals for my life.

_____ 5. I can create the life I desire for myself.

_____ 6. I have the personality traits necessary to achieve the goals I set.

_____ 7. I have unique talents and skills.

_____ 8. I have a support system I can depend on when I need help.

_____ 9. I have the ability to make changes in my life.

_____ 10. I am in control of my life.

_____ 11. I feel good when I have control over others.

_____ 12. I expect to be successful in life.

_____ 13. I am limited in what I can achieve in life because of my race.

_____ 14. I am limited in what I can achieve in life because of my sex (gender).

_____ 15. I can break old habits.

_____ 16. I understand why I take certain actions in life.

_____ 17. I am angry most of the time.

_____ 18. I am taking the actions necessary to improve my life circumstances.

_____ 19. I can handle whatever comes in life.

_____ 20. I can imagine a better life for myself.